D1129595

DISCARDED

DISCARDED

FRANKENSTEIN'S MONSTER

Cathleen Small

Cavendish Square

New York

CREATURES OF FANTASY
FRANKENSTEIN'S MONSTER

BY

Cathleen Small

CAVENDISH SQUARE PUBLISHING · NEW YORK

Published in 2016 by Cavendish Square Publishing, LLC
243 5th Avenue, Suite 136, New York, NY 10016

Copyright © 2016 by Cavendish Square Publishing, LLC

First Edition

No part of this publication may be reproduced, stored in a retrieval system, or transmitted in any form or by any means—electronic, mechanical, photocopying, recording, or otherwise—without the prior permission of the copyright owner. Request for permission should be addressed to Permissions, Cavendish Square Publishing, 243 5th Avenue, Suite 136, New York, NY 10016. Tel (877) 980-4450; fax (877) 980-4454.

Website: cavendishsq.com

This publication represents the opinions and views of the author based on his or her personal experience, knowledge, and research. The information in this book serves as a general guide only. The author and publisher have used their best efforts in preparing this book and disclaim liability rising directly or indirectly from the use and application of this book.

CPSIA Compliance Information: Batch #CW16CSQ

All websites were available and accurate when this book was sent to press.

Cataloging-in-Publication Data

Small, Cathleen.
Frankenstein's monster / by Cathleen Small.
p. cm. — (Creatures of fantasy)
Includes index.
ISBN 978-1-5026-0936-6 (hardcover) ISBN 978-1-5026-0937-3 (ebook)
1. Frankenstein's monster (Fictitious character) — Juvenile literature. 2. Shelley, Mary Wollstonecraft, — 1797-1851. — Frankenstein — Juvenile literature. 3. Frankenstein, Victor (Fictitious character) — Juvenile literature. I. Small, Cathleen. II. Title.
PR5397.F73 S63 2016
823'.7—d23

Editorial Director: David McNamara
Editor: Kristen Susienka
Copy Editor: Nathan Heidelberger
Art Director: Jeffrey Talbot
Designer: Joseph Macri
Senior Production Manager: Jennifer Ryder-Talbot
Production Editor: Renni Johnson
Photo Research: J8 Media

The photographs in this book are used by permission and through the courtesy of: Silver Screen Collection/Getty Images, cover; English School/Look and Learn/Bridgeman Images, 2-3; Hulton Archive/Getty Images, 6, 29, 34; Derrick from Atlanta, Georgia (http://flickr.com/photos/16231096@N00)/ File:Unclestein, experiment-in-the-making.jpg/Wikimedia Commons, 8; AF archive/Alamy, 13, 14, 36; Public Domain/File:Borris Karloff still.jpg/Wikimedia Commons, 16; TriStar/Getty Images, 19; Silver Screen Collection/Getty Images, 20; 20th Century Fox/Archive Photos/Getty Images, 21; Ullstein Bild via Getty Images, 26; Monster of Frankenstein #1 (Jan. 1973) Marvel Comics. Cover art by Mike Ploog both pencils & inks per GCD/ File:MonsterOfFrankenstein1.jpg/Wikimedia Commons, 30; TEK IMAGE/SPL/Getty Images, 32; leoks/Shutterstock.com, 40; Howat, Andrew/Look and Learn/Bridgeman Images, 42; J. D. Dallet Therin-Weise/AGE Fotostock/Getty Images, 45; AsiaDreamPhoto Alamy, 47; TOHO Album Newscom, 48; Photos 12 Alamy, 51; gregobagel/iStockphoto.com, 54; Photos 12 Alamy, 57; Christos Georghiou/Shutterstock.com, 58.

Printed in the United States of America

CONTENTS

Boris Karloff's iconic portrayal of Frankenstein's monster remains a film classic.

INTRODUCTION

Since the first humans walked the earth, myths and legends have engaged minds and inspired imaginations. Ancient civilizations used stories to explain phenomena in the world around them: the weather, tides, and natural disasters. As different cultures evolved, so too did their stories. From their traditions and observations emerged creatures with powerful abilities, mythical intrigue, and their own origins. Sometimes, different cultures encouraged various manifestations of the same creature. At other times, these creatures and cultures morphed into entirely new beings with greater powers than their predecessors.

Today, societies still celebrate the folklore of their ancestors—on-screen in presentations such as *The Hobbit, The Walking Dead,* and *X-Men*; and in stories such as *Harry Potter* and *Twilight*. Some even believe these creatures truly existed and continue to walk the earth as living creatures. Others resign these beings to myth.

In the Creatures of Fantasy series, we celebrate captivating stories of the past from all around the world. Each book focuses on creatures both familiar and unknown: the terrifying ghost, the bloodthirsty vampire, the classic Frankenstein's monster, mischievous goblins, enchanting witches, and the callous zombie. Here their various incarnations throughout history are brought to life. All have their own origins, their own legends, and their own influences on the imagination today. Each story adds a new perspective to the human experience and encourages people to revisit tales of the past in order to understand their presence in the modern age.

THE MYTH OF FRANKENSTEIN'S MONSTER

"It's alive, it's alive, IT'S ALIVE!"

COLIN CLIVE AS HENRY FRANKENSTEIN,

FRANKENSTEIN (UNIVERSAL PICTURES, 1931)

FRANKENSTEIN: A GREEN-SKINNED, SAD-EYED monstrosity with bolts in his neck. That's the image that comes to mind when we hear the name, but just in that one-sentence description there are two myths. First, Frankenstein wasn't the monster's name—it was the name of the doctor who created him. Second, in the original myth, which came to life in Mary Shelley's early-1800s Gothic horror novel *Frankenstein*, there is no description of the monster having green skin or bolts in his neck. Rather, the monster is described as having "yellow skin." However, images stick in our memory, so the green-skinned monster portrayed by actor Boris Karloff in the Frankenstein films of the 1930s is what we think of when we envision the

Opposite: Yet another visual representation of Frankenstein's monster

9

monster. When the films were released—*Frankenstein* in 1931 and *The Bride of Frankenstein* in 1935—they weren't in color. Since then, old films have been colorized, the green skin made visible, and so the on-screen image prevails.

One feature of Frankenstein's monster that has remained true to the book in all adaptations is his height. In the novel he is described as being 8 feet (2.4 meters) tall. While 8 feet isn't *that* outside the norm—some adults are more than 7 feet (2.1 m) tall—it's enough to make the monster appear imposing. Moreover, this depiction has persisted. In media portrayals even today, the monster is indeed quite tall.

FILM VERSUS BOOK

The myth of Frankenstein's monster began with Mary Shelley's novel, but it was furthered by James Whale's 1931 movie. Some people have read the book, some people have seen the movie, some have done both, and some have done neither. Thus, people's perceptions of the monster are influenced by what their exposure to the creature has been.

The beauty of a book is that so much is left to the reader's imagination. Mary Shelley gives a vivid physical description of the monster in the novel, but it takes all of one paragraph, and so it is a small part of the novel. It gives the reader an idea of what the monster looks like, but it's a fluid picture of a yellow-skinned, dark-haired, looming monster with very white teeth. How his hair is styled, the amount of yellow that tints his skin, and what his other features look like are left to the reader's imagination. Is his skin pale with just a hint of yellow, such as a person suffering from jaundice or liver disease, or is the hue more of a dark, bracing

yellow? His hair is described as "flowing," but is it straight? Or curly? Wavy? It's all left to the reader's imagination. Readers know that Dr. Frankenstein finds his creation to be hideous, but beauty is in the eye of the beholder, so how hideous is hideous? In the book, readers can lose themselves in their imagination, conjuring up vivid images of the horrible-looking creature.

However, a movie is a very different story. In a movie, an actor portrays the monster, and he's in full makeup. His black hair appears more close-cropped and oily than the "flowing" hair described in the book. His skin has a green tinge to it. He has Boris Karloff's sad, drooping eyes, and of course, there are the bolts in his neck, which have become a hallmark of portrayals of Frankenstein's creation. A picture is supposedly worth a thousand words, and indeed the picture of Frankenstein's monster from the movie is far more embedded in most people's minds than the short, seventy-nine-word description of him that Mary Shelley provided in the novel. Even those who have read the novel may find their initial conception of the monster's appearance to be replaced by the vivid image of the monster portrayed on film.

Myths into Films

The silver screen has long translated myths into films, sometimes with more success than other times. *Frankenstein* is one example of a myth that was wildly successful both in its original form (in literature) and on the screen. Other myths that were successfully translated into films include *My Fair Lady*, based on the myth of Pygmalion; *Ulysses*, based on the Greek myth of Odysseus, king of Ithaca; and Disney's *Hercules*, based on the Greek **hero**. Then of course there are those films influenced by legends or fairy tales, such as the Leprechaun series of horror films, based on the mythical leprechaun.

From Pages to Screen:
A Loose Adaptation

Frankenstein's monster has been portrayed numerous times in many ways since the novel debuted nearly two hundred years ago. Probably the two best-known portrayals are in Mary Shelley's novel and in the 1931 film adaptation starring Boris Karloff. However, it's important to note that the film is a loose adaptation of the book. For starters, in Shelley's novel, Dr. Victor Frankenstein worked alone on his creation. In fact, his self-imposed isolation is a critical element of the Gothic in Shelley's novel. In the movie, however, *Henry* Frankenstein works with an assistant, Fritz, who happens to be a hunchback. Fritz, as it turns out, accidentally puts the brain of a deceased murderer into the monster's body. Thus, while in the book the monster is solely the creation and responsibility of Frankenstein, in the movie Fritz takes some of the blame—particularly for giving the monster the brain of a murderer.

Also, in the book, Frankenstein flees from the monster the moment he sees life in the creature's eyes. In the movie, Frankenstein is intrigued by the monster at first and invites him to sit down. It is only when the monster is startled by a flaming torch—brought in by Fritz, who once again gets to take the blame—that Frankenstein mistakenly believes the creature is aggressive and chains him in the dungeon. Fritz is left to antagonize the monster with the torch, which frightens the monster into attacking and ultimately killing Fritz.

These changes in plot bring forth an interesting twist in the myth. In Shelley's book, Frankenstein is technically the novel's **protagonist**. However, he's a complicated protagonist because he's really not a hero. Heroes in literature are typically courageous and

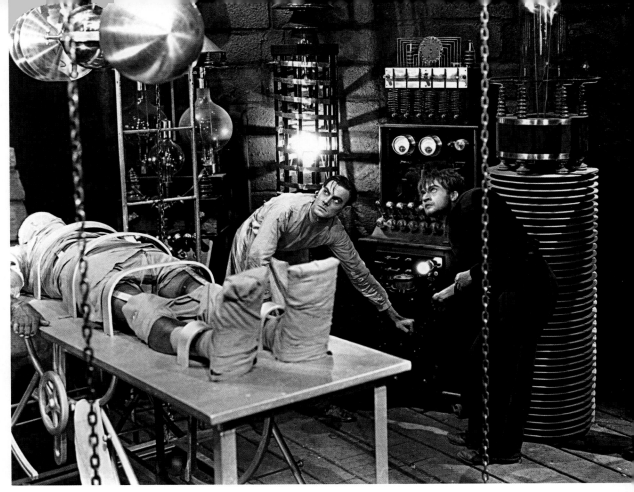

In the 1931 film
Frankenstein,
Henry Frankenstein
and his assistant,
Fritz, bring life to
the monster.

noble, among other positive qualities, and Dr. Frankenstein is a bit of a loathsome character—he creates a monster, gives it life, and then runs from it because he is appalled by its hideousness. The monster is lonely and isolated because his own creator has rejected him. Thus, readers see Dr. Frankenstein as a rather weak, flawed man, not particularly heroic in any way.

In the movie, on the other hand, Frankenstein takes on more of a traditional heroic role because Fritz gets to be the bad guy. After all, he is the one who gives the monster his aggressive tendencies by putting a murderer's brain in his body, and he is the one who spurs the monster to violence by antagonizing him with a torch. In true Hollywood style, the movie version gives viewers a more

Hollywood loves
a good hero and
villain, such as
Batman and
the Joker (in
Batman, 1989).

traditional hero and villain, rather than following the more subtle and complicated character structure of the book.

One factor of the myth that does stay fairly consistent between the book and the movie is that the monster is not immediately aggressive: in both, his murderous acts are motivated by some event. In the novel, the monster murders people in an attempt to get revenge on Dr. Frankenstein for creating him and then abandoning him, forcing the monster to live a life of loneliness and isolation. In the movie, the monster murders people when provoked (as when Fritz antagonizes him with a torch), in an attempt to protect himself (as when the monster murders Dr. Waldman, a former professor of Dr. Frankenstein's, who is about to dissect the monster), or due to a lack of understanding (as when he drowns a young woman because he wants to see if she will float as the flowers on the lake do). This makes the monster a rather complicated villain, too: he is villainous because he murders, but the reasons *why* he murders cause readers and viewers to sympathize with him. Much as Frankenstein is a complicated protagonist, his monster is a complicated villain.

The novel and the movie differ in their endings, too. In the novel, Dr. Frankenstein dies from an illness, and the monster weeps over his body; declares that he, too, can now die; and flees into the Arctic, presumably to die alone—although readers never know whether he really does. In the movie, the monster attempts to murder Frankenstein by throwing him from the top of an old mill but is unsuccessful. Villagers then try to kill the monster by burning the mill, but they, too, are unsuccessful.

Some of the changes in plot points from book to film are minor and relatively inconsequential, but some of them put a strong twist in the original myth as conceived by Mary Shelley.

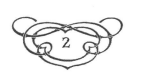
FURTHER REPRESENTATIONS OF THE MONSTER

"Monsters are real, and ghosts are real too.
They live inside us, and sometimes, they win."

STEPHEN KING, AUTHOR

THE TWO MAIN REPRESENTATIONS OF Frankenstein's monster that most people think of are the monster described in Mary Shelley's 1818 novel, *Frankenstein*, and the monster portrayed by Boris Karloff in the 1931 film of the same name. However, those are far from the only depictions of Frankenstein's monster. So iconic is the monster in the Gothic and horror **genres** that he has appeared in many incarnations over the years, in films, television, music, plays, comics, novels, and even video games.

Frankenstein's Monster on the Big Screen

There have been many incarnations of the monster on the big screen. Contrary to popular belief, James Whale's *Frankenstein*

Opposite: Boris Karloff's sad, droopy eyes added to the monster's tragic countenance in the 1931 film.

featuring Boris Karloff as the monster was *not* the first film to showcase the monster. That honor goes to a 1910 film produced by Edison Studios, which ran for a mere sixteen minutes and took liberties with the story. For example, Frankenstein created the monster in a vat rather than out of body parts stolen from corpses. That film was followed by another in 1915, entitled *Life Without Soul,* and also an Italian version released in 1921 with the title *Il Mostro di Frankenstein* (The Monster of Frankenstein). Next came the iconic 1931 film, with Boris Karloff as its star, and soon after, in 1935, came the sequel *The Bride of Frankenstein,* which won critical acclaim and was hugely popular. Capitalizing on its success, Universal Pictures released *Son of Frankenstein* (1939), *The Ghost of Frankenstein* (1942), *Frankenstein Meets the Wolf Man* (1943), *House of Frankenstein* (1944), *House of Dracula* (1945)—the film combined Dracula, the Wolf Man, and Frankenstein's monster in one film— and *Abbott and Costello Meet Frankenstein* (1948). Clearly, the film franchise was quite popular, but it did eventually turn from serious horror films into **B movies**, particularly after *Son of Frankenstein.* In the late 1950s and 1960s, several more films based on the myth of Frankenstein's monster were released in the United States, including *I Was a Teenage Frankenstein* (1958), in which a professor creates the monster out of the parts of dead teenagers killed in a car accident; *Frankenstein 1970* (1958), which delves into nuclear power in its horror theme; *Frankenstein's Daughter* (1958); *Frankenstein Meets the Space Monster* (1965); and *Jesse James Meets Frankenstein's Daughter* (1966), a sci-fi/western mash-up.

Also between the 1950s and early 1970s, British production company Hammer Films produced several movies focusing on Dr. Frankenstein and featuring his monster as part of their

Hammer Horror series. Hammer Films also created a half-hour pilot for a TV series called *Tales of Frankenstein*, but it was never picked up for release.

In the 1970s and 1980s, US film producers seemed to lose their lust for horror films based on Frankenstein's monster, but filmmakers in other countries didn't—there were countless movies featuring the monster created in Europe and Japan, for example. There were a few entries from the United States, though, including the 1985 film *The Bride*, which depicted the monster wandering Europe with a circus midget. Dr. Frankenstein is played by rocker Sting and falls in love with the monster's bride, creating a love triangle between the three. Frankenstein's monster was also featured in the 1987 comedy *The Monster Squad*.

Probably the first serious American film reimagining of Frankenstein's monster after the 1931 version came in 1994, with *Mary Shelley's Frankenstein*. This movie featured Robert De Niro in the role of Frankenstein's monster. It did not stay true to the novel, but it was at least a serious envisioning of the story, rather than a spin-off or a spoof.

A decade later, in 2004, the monster reappeared in the film *Van Helsing*, where he is depicted relatively closely to how the monster is depicted in Mary Shelley's novel (although the film's plot does not follow the novel). Most recently, Frankenstein's monster appeared in the animated film *Hotel Transylvania* (2012), where he was voiced by actor Kevin James.

Robert De Niro portrayed Frankenstein's monster in *Mary Shelley's Frankenstein* (1994).

Frankenstein's Monster on the Small Screen

Frankenstein's monster hasn't only graced the big screen; he has also appeared on the small screen countless times, starting as far back as the early 1950s, when many American homes didn't even have a television set! The first appearance of Frankenstein's monster on the television was in an episode of the 1951–1953 series *Tales of Tomorrow*. The episode featured Lon Chaney Jr. as the monster, which is notable because he also appeared in several 1940s Frankenstein films, including *The Ghost of Frankenstein*, *Frankenstein Meets the Wolf Man*, *House of Frankenstein*, and *Abbott and Costello Meet Frankenstein*. However, a far better known

Fred Gwynne's portrayal of Herman Munster on the TV series *The Munsters* was loosely based on Frankenstein's monster.

representation of the monster on television came in 1964, when CBS debuted *The Munsters*, with character Herman Munster, father of a family of monsters who happened to closely resemble the movie version of Frankenstein's monster. *The Munsters* only ran on CBS for three seasons, but it was a much-loved series, and the Munsters' house is still on display at Universal Studios in California.

Similarly, another 1960s series about a rather bizarre family featured a character who physically resembled Frankenstein's monster. It was called *The Addams Family*, and butler Lurch bore a striking resemblance to the monster.

PARODIES

If the sign of "making it" is becoming the subject of a **parody**, then Frankenstein's monster has definitely made it. The monster has been parodied numerous times, in such films as the Beatles' *Yellow Submarine*, *Young Frankenstein*, and *The Rocky Horror Picture Show*. The 1975 musical parody *The Rocky Horror Picture Show* is a **bawdy** retelling of the myth featuring Dr. Frank N. Furter and his monstrous creation, Rocky. Mel Brooks's 1974 comedy *Young Frankenstein* is a cult classic that played on the first three Frankenstein films produced by Universal in the 1930s. Despite being an irreverent comedy, *Young Frankenstein* has been deemed "culturally, historically or aesthetically significant" by the United States National Film Preservation Board and will be preserved in the Library of Congress's National Film Registry—along with another irreverent Frankenstein-themed film, *The Rocky Horror Picture Show*. It seems parodied versions of Frankenstein's monster are destined for film immortality.

This scence from *Young Frankenstein* (1974) shows actor Gene Wilder playing the grandson of the original Dr. Frankenstein.

So beloved was *The Addams Family* that it spawned several films in the 1990s.

Following that, a number of series featured episodes revolving around themes of the myth of Frankenstein's monster, including *Doctor Who* (in the 1960s and the 1970s), *Dark Shadows* (1968), *Fantasy Island* (1973), and *The X-Files*. A relatively long-running TV series, *Weird Science* (1994–1998), also reimagined the myth of Frankenstein's monster. In it, two teenagers design the perfect woman on their computer, but she is accidentally brought to life after a lightning storm. Cult favorite *Buffy the Vampire Slayer* also featured versions of Frankenstein's monster in episodes in two different seasons, and the long-running animated series *The Simpsons* has featured Frankenstein's monster in at least five episodes. Most recently, the series *Once Upon a Time* has featured a storyline revolving around Dr. Frankenstein and his monster, in which the character, played by David Anders, hopes to raise his deceased brother from the dead.

Even children's television shows have examined the myth of Frankenstein's monster. The popular series *Scooby-Doo* featured the monster in a couple of episodes, as did *Sesame Street*, *Mighty Morphin Power Rangers*, *Animaniacs*, *Robot Chicken*, *Arthur*, *Darkwing Duck*, *The Adventures of Jimmy Neutron: Boy Genius*, *Monster High*, and *SpongeBob SquarePants*.

Frankenstein's Monster in Music

Clearly, the large and small screens have been prime ground for portrayals of the myth of Frankenstein's monster. It stands to reason given that the gruesome physical characteristics of the monster and his tortured nature are compelling to watch—the monster is often

a complicated soul, torn between a kind heart and a frustration at his isolation in society. However, the monster has also found a home in perhaps a less likely place: music.

Probably the most popular representation of Frankenstein's monster in music is in the 1962 song "Monster Mash," performed by Bobby "Boris" Pickett. If you have ever listened to the radio around Halloween then you've undoubtedly heard this tune, which includes the lyrics: *"I was working in the lab late one night / When my eyes beheld an eerie sight / For my monster from his slab began to rise / And suddenly to my surprise / He did the mash / He did the monster mash."*

A more recent song to include the Frankenstein myth is "Weird Al" Yankovic's "Perform This Way," released in 2011. The song is a riff on Lady Gaga's unique style, but it incorporates the Frankenstein myth in the lines: *"Don't be offended when you see / My latest pop monstrosity / I'm strange, weird, shocking, odd, bizarre/ I'm Frankenstein, I'm Avatar."*

However, these aren't the only times Frankenstein's monster has been represented in music. In 1973, the Edgar Winter Group composed "Frankenstein," which they named because they cobbled the instrumental piece together from multiple takes of recording. Another song called "Frankenstein" is by a funk metal band called Clutch and was released in 2001, and yet a *third* song named "Frankenstein" was also released in 2001, this one by metal band Iced Earth. The metal band Helloween released "Dr. Stein," a song based on Frankenstein and his monster, on their 1988 album *Keeper of the Seven Keys, Pt. 2.* These songs aren't terribly well known, but Alice Cooper's 1991 "Feed My Frankenstein" had wider appeal— particularly after being featured in the hit film *Wayne's World.* That wasn't Cooper's first Frankenstein-themed song, though. In 1986,

he recorded "Teenage Frankenstein." Well-known metal band Metallica also featured the myth of Frankenstein's monster in themes from their 2004 song "Some Kind of Monster." In 2005, Christian singer Kevin Max included the song "Jumpstart Your Electric Heart" on this album *The Imposter*; the song reimagines Mary Shelley's story of the monster. Most recently, rock band Glass Wave included the song "Creature" on a 2010 album. In the song, the lyrics are delivered in the creature's voice.

Occasionally, Frankenstein's monster has even been featured in music videos for songs where he wasn't the subject of the music or lyrics. Back in the 1980s, when music videos were quite popular, the monster featured in videos for songs by Sheena Easton, the Dead Milkmen, Yazoo, and Huey Lewis and the News.

Frankenstein's Monster Takes the Stage

Having conquered the large and small screens and the airwaves, it's no surprise that Frankenstein's monster would also appear on the stage. In fact, he did so long before he ever appeared on the screen or the radio. In 1823, the play *Presumption; or, the Fate of Frankenstein* was produced in London, and in 1887, a musical burlesque entitled *Frankenstein, or The Vampire's Victim* was produced.

After that, there was a lull of nearly a century before the next major production involving Frankenstein's monster—and unfortunately, it proved to be a colossal flop. A Broadway play opened in January 1981 and showed for exactly one performance before closing in disgrace. Much more successful was *Young Frankenstein*, a musical theater adaptation debuting in 2007. It was based on the successful Mel Brooks comedic film and ran for close to fifteen months before closing.

Frankenstein's Monster in Fiction

Frankenstein's monster also has a firm place in **fan fiction.** Numerous authors, both American and European, have written sequels to Mary Shelley's original novel or have written original works inspired by Shelley's portrayal of the monster or by the portrayal of the monster in the movies. Authors Brian Aldiss, Robert J. Myers, Allan Rune Pettersson, and Fred Saberhagen have all written such novels. Saberhagen's takes an interesting twist, telling the story from the monster's point of view (where Shelley's novel told the story from a ship captain's point of view, as related to him by Dr. Frankenstein). Probably the best-known authors to tackle the myth of Frankenstein's monster since Mary Shelley are contemporary horror authors Stephen King and Dean Koontz. One of King's most popular novels, *It* (1986), features a monster that at one point takes the form of Frankenstein's monster. Dean Koontz has an entire series of five books called Dean Koontz's Frankenstein that places the myth of Frankenstein's monster in modern-day New Orleans, Louisiana.

Other clever takes on the myth of Frankenstein's monster include *Frankenstein According to Spike Milligan*, a parody that plays on Shelley's novel, and *The Casebook of Victor Frankenstein*, in which Victor Frankenstein encounters Percy Bysshe Shelley, real-life husband of Mary Shelley. Perhaps not surprisingly, Frankenstein's monster has appeared countless times in comics, particularly in those produced by both DC Comics and Marvel.

It's clear that the myth of Frankenstein's monster translates incredibly well to page, stage, and screen. The monster comes to life in any type of media, leaping off the screen or climbing off the pages, his ghastly skin and yellowed eyes always ready to scare and delight.

THE MONSTER'S POWERS

"Ever since I've been a little kid, I've always wanted superpowers, which is the coolest thing in the world."

ALEXANDER LUDWIG, ACTOR

ONE CHARACTERISTIC OF MYTHICAL creatures is that they are typically imbued with some sort of magical powers—sometimes good, and sometimes evil. For example, basilisks are said to be able to cause death to anyone who gazes upon them, leprechauns can grant wishes, and the horn of a unicorn is said to have strong medicinal powers. Similarly, the mythical monster created by Frankenstein is said to have powers, though his powers depend on the particular portrayal of the monster.

Opposite: This scene from *Frankenstein* (1931) shows Boris Karloff's version of the monster to be very tall.

The Power of the Spoken Word

The original monster in Mary Shelley's novel is portrayed as being extremely eloquent. He doesn't come by his articulateness

naturally, though. He learns to talk by listening to a family speak while he is hiding out and by reading discarded books he has found. His aptitude for learning is not surprising, though, as the monster is described as having a large brain and learning voraciously. In one pivotal plot point, the monster despairs when Dr. Frankenstein destroys a second creature he has made to be the monster's companion. We understand the monster's frustration and sorrow; we expect his frustration and rage, but what is unexpected is the eloquence with which the monster expresses his dismay:

> You have destroyed the work which you began; what is it that you intend? Do you dare to break your promise? I have endured toil and misery; I left Switzerland with you; I crept along the shores of the Rhine, among its willow islands and over the summits of its hills. I have dwelt many months in the heaths of England and among the deserts of Scotland. I have endured incalculable fatigue, and cold, and hunger; do you dare destroy my hopes?

The monster goes on to deliver an eloquent threat to Dr. Frankenstein that he will be with him on his wedding night.

Words and eloquence are not a mythical power, to be sure, but they are powerful nonetheless. With his articulate speech, the monster has gained a reader's sympathy and inflicted guilt and fear on Dr. Frankenstein. Words can be a sword, and the monster wields a powerful one.

The Powers of Strength and Speed

In the novel and in the movie versions depicting Frankenstein's monster, he is both strong and fast. His joints are described as "more supple" than those of an average man. He moves quickly throughout the countryside when he needs to, and his strength allows him to kill swiftly when enraged. It stands to reason that he would be strong, though, as he is described in the book as being quite large—around 8 feet (2.4 m) tall—and in the movies he is similarly depicted. In the 1930s movies in which Frankenstein's monster was portrayed by Boris Karloff, the monster is also indestructible.

In the 1931 *Frankenstein* movie, the monster is indestructible—even at the hands of an angry mob.

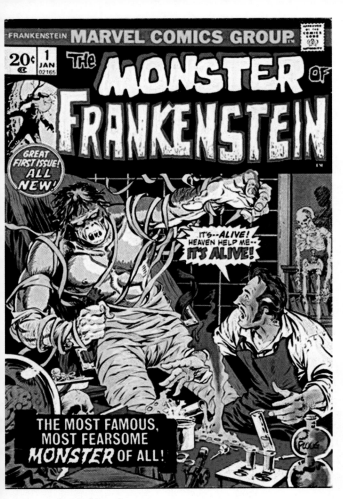

In his Marvel Comics portrayal, the monster is invincible and does not age.

Whether because of his size, his speed, magical power, or simply the magic of Hollywood, the villagers who attempt to kill the monster are no match for the creature.

The Power of Death

In many representations of the myth, Frankenstein's monster was created from the body parts of dead people. This often makes the monster not susceptible to many of the weaknesses of other human beings. For instance, in many representations, the monster doesn't feel pain, he doesn't need food or other **sustenance**, and he doesn't need rest. If he loses a body part, he can simply replace it with a similar body part from another corpse. In the DC Comics versions of Frankenstein's monster, the fact that he is composed of body parts from dead people makes him physically invincible, unnaturally strong, and functionally **immortal**. The same holds true in Marvel Comics' representations, although in Marvel Comics he also does not age.

Marvel Comics imbued Frankenstein's monster with a few extra abilities and powers, too. Marvel's version of the monster is excellent at hand-to-hand combat, but all self-taught, through a century of experience. He is an expert in the **occult** because he has encountered many supernatural beings during his existence. Furthermore, he is able to regenerate, or heal when he is injured. However, he does have some weaknesses—namely, he is vulnerable to extremes in temperature.

Power can come in many forms, but like many other mythical creatures, Frankenstein's monster is imbued with a number of different powers—some intellectual and some physical. What those are and how they are manifested depends on the version of the myth you consult.

Regenerative Healing: Reality vs. Fiction

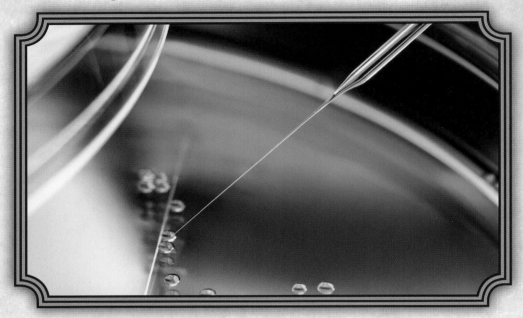

Regeneration *sounds* like something out of a supernatural novel, doesn't it? Get shot and watch the bullet hole in your chest magically seal up, good as new. However, in reality, this isn't entirely myth. There is a branch of medical research that focuses on regenerative medicine. The well-respected Mayo Clinic describes regenerative medicine as "a game-changing area of medicine with the potential to fully heal damaged tissues and organs, offering solutions and hope for people who have conditions that today are beyond repair." Regenerative healing involves using specific types of cells or cell products to help diseased tissues and organs repair themselves.

Above: Regenerative healing was a myth in Mary Shelley's *Frankenstein*, but it's not anymore.

Bone marrow transplants are a good example of regenerative healing—when a patient has diseased bone marrow (from certain types of cancers, for example), sometimes healthy marrow can be transplanted into the person's bones and can take over and begin to produce new healthy marrow, replacing the diseased marrow.

You may have heard of the term **stem-cell research**. This is a key component of regenerative medicine. Stem cells can be used in regenerative medicine to treat such conditions as diabetes, heart failure, and degenerative nerve, bone, and joint conditions. However, there is controversy attached to the practice because of the ways some stem cells are harvested. A particular type of stem cell, called a **human embryonic stem cell**, is extremely useful in medical applications because all kinds of tissues in the human body originate from this particular type of stem cell. In other words, there's a lot in that tiny package. However, that tiny package is obtained in one way: from human embryos left over from assisted reproduction attempts, such as in vitro fertilization. In other words, to obtain the human embryonic stem cells, the embryos—ones that are not implanted in a mother—are destroyed, and to some people, that is essentially taking a human life. You can see the ethical debate that arises, then: there are potential medical gains to be made, but a cost at which they may come.

Further complicating the issue is the fact that this subject is fraught with conflicting information. Some sources insist that human embryonic stem cells can be obtained without destroying the embryo, and others insist that this is not true. So, much like the ethical debate in robbing graves to "create" a human, there is debate in robbing human lives in the name of science.

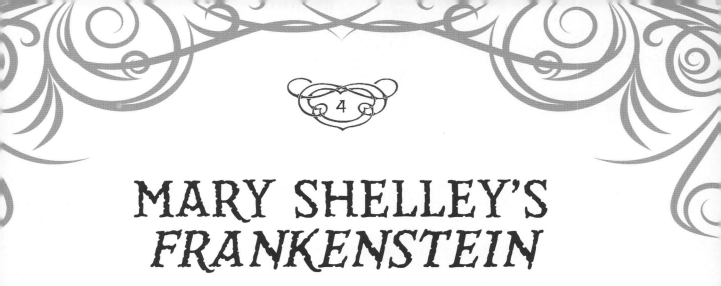

MARY SHELLEY'S
FRANKENSTEIN

"I beheld the wretch—the miserable monster whom I had created. He held up the curtain of the bed; and his eyes, if eyes they may be called, were fixed on me. His jaws opened, and he muttered some inarticulate sounds, while a grin wrinkled his cheeks. He might have spoken, but I did not hear; one hand was stretched out, seemingly to detain me, but I escaped and rushed downstairs."

DR. VICTOR FRANKENSTEIN, *FRANKENSTEIN* (1818)

THE MYTH OF FRANKENSTEIN'S MONSTER has been around for nearly two hundred years, since a novel called *Frankenstein; or, the Modern Prometheus* was published anonymously in London in 1818. Five years later, when a second edition of the novel was published in France, the world learned who the author was: Mary Wollstonecraft Shelley, daughter of famous feminist Mary Wollstonecraft and wife of **Romantic** poet Percy Bysshe Shelley.

The idea for *Frankenstein* came to Shelley while she was spending the summer in Geneva, Switzerland, with her stepsister, her stepsister's lover (poet Lord Byron), and Percy Bysshe Shelley, who later became Mary's husband. The foursome were trapped in the house by bad

Opposite: A portrait of Mary Shelley, the creator of the original myth of Frankenstein's monster

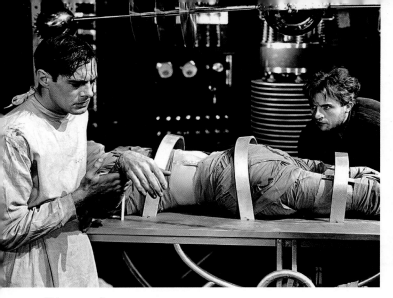

This scene from *Frankenstein* (1931) shows actors Colin Clive and Dwight Frye as lead characters.

weather at one point, and they began reading ghost stories. An informal contest ensued, with the writers competing to see who could write the best ghost story. Mary won with her creepy tale of Dr. Frankenstein and the monster he created.

Interestingly, although the name "Frankenstein" is often believed to describe the monster, in reality, Victor Frankenstein was the *creator* of the monster in Mary Shelley's novel. The actual monster has no name; it is simply known as the Creature or Frankenstein's monster. Because it is vague and somewhat confusing to simply refer to "the monster" or "the creature" when you want to speak specifically of the monster created by Frankenstein, and because it's a bit of a mouthful to always refer to "Frankenstein's monster," over the years people have shortened the monster's descriptive name to simply "Frankenstein"—regardless of the name being inaccurate.

The Novel That Started It All

Unlike many Gothic novels, Mary Shelley's *Frankenstein* is not a long book; depending on the edition, it generally runs about 150 pages. However, what it lacks in length, it makes up for in creepiness. The novel is divided into three volumes. In Volume I, an English ship captain named Robert Walton writes a series of letters to his sister as he sails to the North Pole. When his ship gets stuck in the Arctic ice, Walton takes a disheveled man on board: Victor Frankenstein. Frankenstein tells Walton the story of a monster he is pursuing, and Walton in turn relates this tale to his sister through his letters.

The monster, of course, is Dr. Frankenstein's own creation. As a university student, Frankenstein was fascinated by **alchemy**, philosophy, and chemistry, and after much study, eventually he determines that he has discovered the secret of life. With this information, Frankenstein decides to create a new race of beings. He then spends months making a creature out of old human body parts, but when he brings the creature to life on a dark November night, Frankenstein is horrified by his creation and flees from it.

Not long after, Frankenstein learns that his brother has been murdered. On his way home to pay his respects, Frankenstein sees his monster and assumes that the monster must have murdered his brother, William. However, no one else knows about Frankenstein's suspicions, and Justine, a girl who had been adopted by Frankenstein's family, is tried and convicted for William's murder, and she is executed.

At that point, Frankenstein feels responsible for two deaths—William's and Justine's—given that he created the monster who he believes murdered William and led to Justine's conviction and death. In Volume II, Frankenstein escapes to a vacation, hoping to assuage his guilty conscience, and he once again runs into his monster. The monster admits that he killed William and says it was an act of revenge toward Frankenstein, who created him and then cruelly abandoned him. He fills Frankenstein in on his lonely existence and the multiple times he attempted to connect with people but was cruelly shunned. William, who calls him a "hideous monster," is the last straw—Frankenstein's monster kills William and frames Justine for the murder. The monster, lonely in his isolation, begs Frankenstein to create a mate for him. Frankenstein insists that he will do so only if the monster then leaves Europe forever.

In Volume III, Frankenstein tries to delay creating a mate for the monster, so afraid is he that the two will mate and create "a race of devils." He eventually fulfills his promise and begins to build a female monster, but just before she is finished, Frankenstein destroys her—he cannot get past his anxiety about creating another such monster. The monster sees what Frankenstein has done and vows to be "with [him] on [his] wedding-night."

Eventually, when Frankenstein marries Elizabeth, a young woman whom his family had adopted as a child, he is mindful of the monster's warning and fears that he will be killed on his wedding night. To protect Elizabeth, he sends her away temporarily—but when he hears Elizabeth's screams, he realizes that the monster has killed his wife, not him. Determined to get revenge, Frankenstein begins to track and follow the monster, which is how he ends up running into Captain Walton's ship in the Arctic—he was in pursuit of the monster, and a break in the Arctic ice left a gap between them.

While on the ship with Walton, Frankenstein falls ill and dies. Walton enters the room where Frankenstein's body lies and sees the monster weeping. The monster professes to be lonely and miserable and says that now that his cruel creator has died, he, too, can die. The monster exits through the window, and there Shelley's novel ends.

Dr. Frankenstein's Monster

Frankenstein's monster, as described in Shelley's novel, was a large creature. As Frankenstein relates the story of creating the monster (told by Captain Walton in letters to his sister), he describes how he "began the creation of a human being ... of a gigantic stature, that is to say, about eight feet in height, and proportionally large."

The reason for the creature's size is because smaller body parts hindered Frankenstein's speed in actually building the creature.

Frankenstein had gleaned his ideas about the secret of life in part by studying the decay of bodies in graveyards, and it is graveyards and slaughterhouses where he returns to harvest many of the body parts he uses to create the monster:

> Who shall conceive the horrors of my secret toil as I dabbled among the unhallowed damps of the grave or tortured the living animal to animate the lifeless clay? ... I collected bones from **charnel-houses** and disturbed, with profane fingers, the tremendous secrets of the human frame. In a solitary chamber, or rather cell, at the top of the house ... I kept my workshop of filthy creation ... The dissecting room and the slaughter-house furnished many of my materials.

Frankenstein toils feverishly for nearly two years on his creation, but on a dark November night, when it is time to finally bring the creature to life, he is disgusted by what he has wrought. Frankenstein describes the "breathless horror and disgust" that fills his heart when the beauty of his two-year dream is replaced by revulsion at the creature, of whom he says "a mummy again endued with animation could not be so hideous as that wretch." He contemplates that the unfinished creature was ugly, but when his body was animated with life, the creature "became a thing such as Dante could not have conceived [in his description of hell in his fourteenth-century epic poem]." So devastated is Frankenstein that he flees and becomes extremely ill, and so is confined for several months.

Gothic Literature

Castles are often prime settings for Gothic novels.

Gothicism became a literary genre in the late eighteenth century, falling within the larger category of Romantic literature. However, Romantic literature was quite formal and structured, and Gothic literature was quite the opposite. Initially, Gothic novels often contained plots detailing terrifying experiences usually occurring in ancient castles. Castles, after all, were great settings for unnerving tales, with their underground dungeons, secret passages, and graveyards. As the genre progressed, it came to encompass novels about the **macabre**, the supernatural, the terrifying, and the mysterious. Setting, however, was always important. Even if the novel didn't take place inside a castle, the setting was a critical plot device consisting of some sort of crumbling, decaying structure or scenery that evoked a creepy feeling and was indicative of the decay of a once-thriving location.

The protagonist in a Gothic novel is usually isolated in some way, whether voluntarily or involuntarily, and the villain is usually evil due to a fall from grace or from implied **malevolence**. There is often a wanderer in Gothic novels who travels the world in exile. Such is the case with the monster in Mary Shelley's *Frankenstein*. It becomes difficult to tell who is truly the protagonist in Shelley's novel and who is the villain: both Frankenstein and his monster are isolated—one voluntarily (Frankenstein) and one involuntarily (his monster, who longs to connect with someone). Although the murderous monster is the obvious villain, Frankenstein himself is a villain as well, having fallen from grace by creating the monster and then abandoning him, which is the catalyst that turns the monster into a murderer. The fluidity in who is the protagonist and who is the villain is certainly in contrast to the rigid traditions of Romantic literature and is part of what earns Shelley's novel its well-deserved reputation as a masterpiece of Gothic literature.

For a time, Gothic literature was the most popular genre of fiction in England. Mary Shelley's *Frankenstein* is often considered the most enduring Gothic novel of the time and "the single most important product of the Gothic tradition," but other famous authors from that era include Jane Austen (whose first novel was *Northanger Abbey*, a Gothic spoof, but whose later books were not Gothic in nature) and Ann Radcliffe, a bestselling novelist and "Queen of Terror" whose Gothic novels included 1794's *The Mysteries of Udolpho* and 1797's *The Italian*. The Gothic literary genre has endured and still exists today. The current best-known Gothic author? Stephen King.

THE MONSTER AND GRAVE ROBBING

"There is something at work in my soul which I do not understand. I am practically industrious ... but besides this there is a love for the marvelous, a belief in the marvelous, intertwined in all my projects ... even to the wild sea and unvisited regions I am about to explore."

DR. VICTOR FRANKENSTEIN, *FRANKENSTEIN* (1818)

IN 1818, MARY SHELLEY'S TALE WAS delightfully ghoulish: a young doctor becomes crazed by his desire to harness the secret of life and create a human being. To understand how to do so, he studies corpses because "to examine the causes of life, we must first have recourse to death." Dr. Frankenstein explains that he has never been squeamish regarding matters of death and decay and describes his observations with almost passionate reverence:

I paused, examining and analysing [*sic*] all the minutiae of causation, as exemplified in the change from life to death, and death to life, until from the midst of this darkness a

Opposite: William Burke and William Hare were probably the most famous body snatchers.

sudden light broke in upon me—a light so brilliant and wondrous, yet so simple, that while I became dizzy with the immensity of the prospect which it illustrated, I was surprised that among so many men of genius who had directed their inquiries towards the same science, that I alone should be reserved to discover so astonishing a secret.

Dr. Frankenstein is enthralled by death and all its possibilities—what it means for his study of life. For him, there is no fear in death, only possibility. He begins collecting body parts from these corpses to build his creature. To readers, it is delightfully macabre. However, this fanciful tale isn't really as far from the truth as it might seem. **Grave robbing** was (and occasionally still is) an actual issue. Grave robbing has gone on for centuries and usually occurs for one of two reasons: to steal artifacts from the deceased's tomb or to steal the deceased's body. The latter is often also referred to as **body snatching**.

Tomb Raiders

Believe it or not, grave robbing was an issue even as far back as ancient Egypt. During that time, the motive was mostly to steal valuables. In ancient Egypt, people were buried with their valuables, which included jewelry, gold, silver, and weapons, so teams of grave robbers would break into tombs, remove the fabric from around a mummified corpse, and look for valuables.

The Egyptians believed that the tomb contained the two parts of the deceased person's soul, and that every night the two parts of the soul returned to the person's body and tomb. Thus, if the wrapped body was disturbed or the tomb was broken, the Egyptians

felt that the two parts of the soul were unable to return to the body and the deceased person would lose his afterlife. Breaking into a tomb—and, by association,

Egyptian tombs like this one were raided by grave robbers.

grave robbing—was an unforgivable offense punishable by death by impalement or being burned alive.

The Burke and Hare Murders

Two well-known body snatchers were active in Edinburgh, Scotland, about a decade after Mary Shelley's novel was published. Their names were William Burke and William Hare, and they were Irish immigrants.

Burke and Hare weren't body snatchers in the strictest sense of the term: they didn't rob graves for corpses. Instead, they specialized in fresh corpses—they killed their victims and then immediately sold them to Dr. Robert Knox, who used them as dissection subjects for his anatomy lectures. Their method for obtaining bodies and their purposes for the bodies classifies them as **anatomy murderers**. However, their gruesome business venture didn't start out quite that diabolically. Their first sale was of an old retiree from the army who died of natural causes but owed Hare rent money. To recoup the money, Hare and his friend Burke took the body to Edinburgh University to look for a buyer for the corpse. They received nearly double the amount owed in rent (£4) and walked away with more than £7 (more than $1,100 US in 2015). This handsome profit made them greedy for more, so they suffocated a sick tenant and sold his body. Then they lured in a victim from the streets. This went on for the better part of ten months, until a couple of lodgers grew suspicious and found a body underneath a bed in the Hare home, which ultimately resulted in the arrest of both Burke and Hare. In total, they are said to have sold Knox sixteen corpses. Perhaps most startling may be Burke and Hare's accomplices in this scheme: Hare's wife, Margaret, and Burke's mistress, Helen McDougal.

Wondering why Robert Knox was in the market for corpses for his anatomy lectures? In the early 1800s, there weren't enough cadavers available for the number of anatomy lectures in Britain's medical schools. It was a simple issue of supply and demand. The medical schools had previously gotten their cadavers from executions of criminals, but there weren't as many criminals being executed during that time.

Stranger Than Fiction

Some famous people have been stolen from their graves. For example, in a bold grave robbing attempt in 1876, a crew of four counterfeiters attempted to steal Abraham Lincoln's body from its grave in order to claim a ransom. They were foiled by a police informant. In 1977, a reported potential grave robbing of rock star Elvis Presley's body led his family to have it moved from Forest Hills Cemetery in Memphis, Tennessee, to the Presley estate, Graceland. It is unknown whether the plot to rob Presley's grave would've succeeded, but now his body lies safely at Graceland, where the grave is a popular tourist attraction. Another notable example is silent-film star Charlie Chaplin, whose body was stolen from its grave in 1978 by grave robbers who hoped to get a ransom for the stolen body. (Chaplin's widow refused to pay, claiming that the deceased star would've found it "ridiculous.") The grave robbers were arrested, none the richer. A similar situation

occurred in 2001, with the body of Enrico Cuccia, a rich Italian bank president. Once again, the grave robber was caught and arrested.

However, grave robbing isn't just for the rich and famous. In 1991, Susan Alamo's body was removed from its grave, where it had lain for almost seven years. Alamo was the wife of cult leader Tony Alamo, the former head of Alamo Christian Foundation, and she had died in 1982. For the first eighteen months after her death, Tony kept her embalmed corpse on display in his Arkansas compound for church followers, telling them that she was going to rise from the dead. Eventually, he moved the body to a mausoleum he had built on the property, but anticipating a federal raid of the compound in 1991, Alamo's followers fled and Susan's body mysteriously disappeared. It was later determined that Tony Alamo was responsible for his wife's body's disappearance.

Grave robbing may sound like the stuff of creepy horror movies, but really—you can't make this stuff up!

Funeral rituals on Sulawesi are elaborate.

It's All About the Context

Digging up a dead body sounds downright creepy to most of us, but it's not at all creepy if you live on Indonesia's Sulawesi Island, where a local ritual is to **exhume** the body of a mummified, deceased ancestor every three years, clean out the grave, put a new outfit on the corpse, and take it for a walk around the village before reburying it. To the villagers, it's a way of remembering and honoring the dead.

FRANKENSTEIN'S MONSTER AROUND THE WORLD

"The first thing is that I love monsters. I identify with monsters."

GUILLERMO DEL TORO, ACTOR

MARY SHELLEY'S *FRANKENSTEIN* WAS published in England. The initial draft was written while she vacationed in Switzerland, and a second edition was published five years after the first, in France. So, it's safe to say that the original myth of Frankenstein's monster has its roots in England and Europe. However, the myth had worldwide appeal and has spread all over. It became wildly popular in the United States as well, particularly with the release of the *Frankenstein* films by Universal Pictures in the 1930s. Film versions of the myth also had a resurgence in popularity in the United Kingdom in the 1950s, with the Hammer series of films. However, the popularity

Opposite: A still image from Japan's Frankenstein Conquers the World

didn't stop there; the myth of Frankenstein's monster spread to other countries as well.

The Myth in Japan

Japan has a special-effects film genre known as *kaiju*, which translates to "monster." They use many different monsters in these types of films. Godzilla is a particularly well-known example of a monster in Japanese kaiju films. Frankenstein's monster, too, appeared in a kaiju film called *Frankenstein Conquers the World* (1965). The film opens in Nazi Germany and takes place during late World War II, when the Japanese steal the heart of Frankenstein's monster and take it back to Japan to experiment on it. Unfortunately, the heart explodes in the bombing of Hiroshima, and scientists assume it is lost for good—forgetting that the mythical creature's powers include immortality. Thus, the monster returns in the body of a **feral** boy. It's an interesting twist on the original myth. This film spawned a sequel, *Frankenstein's Monsters: Sanda versus Gaira* (known in the United States as *The War of the Gargantuas*), in which two giant incarnations of Frankenstein's monster live in Japan—a violent one in the sea, and a docile one in the mountains. Both creatures were said to be created from the cells of the monster in *Frankenstein Conquers the World*.

Kaiju filmmakers also had plans for a *Frankenstein vs. Godzilla* film, though it was ultimately never made. However, it wasn't the only failed attempt at a Japanese film depicting the myth of Frankenstein's monster. One of the first Japanese attempts to bring Frankenstein's monster to life on screen was in *Frankenstein vs. the Human Vapour*. Unfortunately, that film was also never made.

In 1981, yet another movie depicting this myth of Frankenstein's monster was made. This one, *Kyôfu Densetsu Kaiki! Frankenstein*, was based on both Mary Shelley's novel and the Marvel comic book portrayal of the monster. It exists in a dubbed United States version without a title, but it's informally known as *Monster of Frankenstein* or *Frankenstein Legend of Terror*.

Film is not the only Japanese media to feature the monster. He also appears on television in the **anime** series *Argento Soma*, which aired from 2000 to 2001, and in the 2008 Japanese live-action television series *Kamen Rider Kiva*. Similarly, the monster has had a role in a Japanese **manga** series called *Dragon Ball*.

A still image from Japan's anime series *Dragon Ball Z*

The Myth Across the Pond

The myth of Frankenstein's monster started in Europe, with Mary Shelley writing it in Switzerland and publishing it in England and then France; however, cinematically, it also spread to Europe. In 1968, the BBC series *Mystery and Imagination* adapted the myth and had actor Ian Holm portray both Dr. Frankenstein and the monster. However, that wasn't the first portrayal of the myth on the small screen in the United Kingdom. The long-running show *Doctor Who* has featured the monster on multiple occasions, the first one being in a 1965 episode called "The Chase." In 1971, an Italian film called *La Figlia di Frankenstein* (The Daughter of Frankenstein), in which the monster kills Frankenstein, but Frankenstein's daughter goes on to create a creature from the body of a handsome young man and the brain of an intelligent but unattractive man. One year later, Spanish filmmaker Jesús Franco released *Dracula Contra Frankenstein (Dracula vs. Frankenstein)*, which focused more on Frankenstein than on the monster, but he followed it up quickly with *The Erotic Rights of Frankenstein*, in which an evil count wants to use Frankenstein's monster to help him rule the world. That same year, Italy released another film called *Frankenstein 80*, in which the monster, called Mosaico, is made homicidal because his body constantly rejects the parts from which it's made. In 1973, American artist Andy Warhol produced an Italian-French horror film called *Andy Warhol's Frankenstein* (or *Flesh for Frankenstein*), which used 3-D technology to show gruesome scenes of organ **disembowelment**. There was a bit of a lull in European or British films inspired by the myth of Frankenstein's monster in the 1980s and 1990s, save for a 1984 BBC version of the myth starring actor David Warner as the monster. In 2011, the BBC broadcast the musical drama *Frankenstein's Wedding: Live in Leeds.*

It's clear that Frankenstein's monster is a myth that has nearly universal appeal. From Japan to Europe to the United States, and from novels to films to comic books, the legend of the monster endures.

Frankenstein's Monster in Graphic Art

Representations of Frankenstein's monster have appeared around the world in books, movies, and television shows, but they also have appeared widely in comic books. DC Comics and Marvel Comics, both major comic publishers, have featured Frankenstein's monster too many times to count. In DC Comics, the monster's appearance goes as far back as 1939, when he was featured in an eight-page adaptation of the film *Son of Frankenstein*. In Marvel Comics, the monster first appeared in 1968, when he was cast as an opponent to the X-Men. Smaller comic publishers also printed versions of the myth—and not just in the United States. French comic publisher Aredit had seven issues of its *Hallucinations* comic adopt the Frankenstein's monster myth as envisioned by Jean-Claude Carrière in his novels, all of which were inspired by Shelley's story. In 2009, Papercutz published a version of French cartoonist Marion Mousse's three-volume French graphic novel adaptation of Mary Shelley's *Frankenstein*. In Japan, *The Junji Ito Horror Comic Collection* was a manga adaptation of the novel. *Soul Eater* and *Embalming–The Another Tale of Frankenstein* were two other manga imaginings of the myth.

Don't think the United States was resting on its laurels, though. While France and Japan were publishing these comics and graphic novels representing the myth of the monster, small United States publishers were also featuring the monster in comics. Dark Horse Comics issued a comic version of the 1931 film in 1991, and the Wachowski brothers released the comic series *Doc Frankenstein* in 2004. The following year, Dead Dog Comics produced *Frankenstein: Monster Mayhem* and Speakeasy Comics produced *The Living and the Dead*. In 2006, Big Bang Comics featured Super Frankenstein, a superhero version of the mythical monster.

THE ENDURING MYTH OF THE MONSTER

*"If a character's totally unsympathetic, they're not real and I'm not interested.
Even the real monsters have to have a spark of something you can relate to."*

MATTHEW MACFADYEN, ACTOR

I
T'S BEEN NEARLY TWO HUNDRED YEARS since Mary Shelley wrote her iconic Gothic horror novel, and it's been close to ninety years since Universal released the first *Frankenstein* film in the United States, yet the romance of the myth hasn't worn off. The tale of Frankenstein's monster is still as creepy as it once was, and people still love the chill that comes with imagining a creature made of the parts of dead bodies.

Happy Halloween!

The monster's universal appeal means that he is still ubiquitous in pop culture. Come Halloween, Frankenstein-themed decorations abound, with the monster's gloomy visage and soulless eyes

Opposite: Frankenstein's monster decorations feature prominently around Halloween.

staring from posters and wall decorations. Children dress up as Frankenstein's monster and listen to songs like "Monster Mash," celebrating the ghouls and goblins of the season. In a way, Halloween is the monster's day! It's a day when all things creepy are celebrated, and the undead are an object of fascination.

RETRO TELEVISION

Television shows like *The Munsters* and *The Addams Family* may be decades old, but they're still well loved and watched by new generations on DVD or on streaming services such as Netflix and Hulu. These classic series, both featuring characters based on Frankenstein's monster, have been given reboots, too. Versions of both have shown up in more recent cartoon series and in motion pictures. The first Addams Family movie made its debut on the big screen in 1991. It was later followed by *Addams Family Values* (1993) and *Addams Family Reunion* (1998).

Music videos aren't the popular draw that they were back in the 1980s and 1990s, but Michael Jackson's "Thriller" video is a classic that has been viewed literally millions of times and is particularly popular around Halloween. (One version of the video on YouTube shows more than 251 million views, ranking it among the most popular music videos ever released. Check it out on YouTube if you haven't seen it for a fun blast from the past.) Among the cast of dancing undead in the video are several monstrous creatures bearing similarities to Frankenstein's monster.

CURRENT HOLLYWOOD

The myth of Frankenstein's monster has been referenced more times than can be covered in this book in movies, television, and books,

and several of those reimaginings are relatively recent. A particularly recent version of the myth appears in Disney's 2012 release of Tim Burton's *Frankenweenie*. Tim Burton is known for his surreal, fantastical films, and *Frankenweenie* is no exception. It's a **stop-motion** animation retelling and parody of the 1931 *Frankenstein* movie. In the movie, Victor Frankenstein is a child, and the monster is his dog, Sparky, who is killed by a car while chasing Victor's home run baseball into the street. Victor brings Sparky back to life and is then persuaded by other children to raise other pets from the dead.

Tim Burton reimagined Frankenstein's monster in his 2012 film *Frankenweenie*.

The Monster's Appeal

So why is the monster's appeal so universal and widespread? Why do people still love to experience the myth two hundred years after its initial appearance? Why is the myth so beloved in cultures around the world? The answer likely has two parts. First, people love a good creepy story, and Frankenstein's monster certainly fits the bill: A hideous, murderous monster created from the parts of dead people? There's not much creepier than that. The second part lies in the monster's depth. Frankenstein's monster is a complicated creature. What makes him who he is depends on the version of the myth, but in most cases, he is a lonely, tortured soul who is turned murderous out of despair.

Some representations of the monster look decidedly cheerful!

When characters are just simply bad, they're not as interesting. They may make decent villains, but they're not as interesting as a truly deep, conflicted, multifaceted villain. With Frankenstein's monster, there are so many layers that make up the myth and that contribute to how he becomes a murderous creature that we alternate between feeling sorry for him, wanting him to find happiness, and despising him for his deplorable acts. Yet there's something tantalizing about that range of emotions that the monster evokes.

In short, the monster is a villain about whom it's "fun" to feel conflicted. People are scared of him, people love him, people hate him … and people love to hate him. With the myth of a character that complex, the possibilities for storytelling are endless.

The Reality of the Myth in the Modern Day

It's all fun and games to look at the portrayals of Frankenstein's monster in pop culture today, but there is an element of truth in the myth, too. The story of a passionate scientist robbing graves to use the parts of dead people to create life may have been 100 percent myth in Mary Shelley's day, but it's not 100 percent myth now.

It's true that we no longer resort to grave robbing, but we do take body parts from deceased people and use them to restore life. We simply call it **organ transplant**. Think about it: A person is mortally injured in a car accident, for example, and is brought into the emergency room on life support. It is determined that the person is for all intents and purposes dead, but the organs are still functioning because of life support. If that person has decided to be an organ donor, doctors harvest, or collect, the organs, find a matching recipient who is in need of a particular organ, and start the transplant process. If the process goes well, the deceased person's heart, liver, lungs, kidneys, or even corneas can be transplanted into a person who, without the transplant, might die in the relatively near future, and that person can go on to live a healthy life. It's interesting to consider that what was once macabre in Mary Shelley's day has actually, in some form, become commonplace in the modern world!

Glossary

alchemy A medieval form of chemistry that dealt with the transformation of matter.

anatomy murderers People who murder others to use their bodies for medical research.

anime A style of Japanese animation.

bawdy Dealing with indecent matters in a comical manner.

B movies Lower-budget movies that are not given theater debuts.

body snatching Secretly exhuming bodies from graves, usually to sell the corpses for medical use.

charnel houses Buildings or vaults where corpses or bones are stored.

disembowelment The removal of the internal organs from a person or animal.

exhume To remove a corpse from a grave.

fan fiction Fiction based off an original work and written by fans of the work.

feral Like a wild animal, or in a wild state.

genre A category of artistic composition.

grave robbing The act of robbing a grave to steal either personal effects or the body itself.

hero A person in a story who is typically courageous, noble, and admired.

human embryonic stem cell Stem cells taken from an early-stage embryo that has not yet implanted in a uterus.

immortal Able to live forever.

macabre Horrifying or disturbing because it deals with death or serious injury.

malevolence Wishing to do evil to others.

manga A Japanese style of comic books and graphic novels.

occult Beliefs and practices rooted in the supernatural or mystical.

organ transplant Placing a healthy organ from one person into another person.

parody An imitation of an artist's work with exaggeration for humorous effect.

protagonist A leading character in a work of literature, film, or other fictional piece.

Romantic A period of artistic, literary, and intellectual growth in Europe that emphasized beauty, aesthetics, and emotions. The Romantic period is roughly defined from the late 1700s to the mid-1800s.

stem-cell research Research on how stem cells can be used to help treat certain medical conditions.

stop-motion A type of animation in which an object is physically moved in very small increments between individually photographed frames. When the frames are played in series, the object then appears to move.

sustenance Food or drink that nourishes and provides strength.

To Learn More About Frankenstein's Monster

Books

Hitchcock, Susan Tyler. *Frankenstein: A Cultural History*. New York: W.W. Norton & Company, 2007.

Hoobler, Dorothy. *The Monsters: Mary Shelley and the Curse of Frankenstein*. New York: Back Bay Books, 2007.

Shelley, Mary. *Frankenstein*. Mineola, NY: Dover Publications, 1994.

Website

The Monster in Frankenstein
www.shmoop.com/frankenstein/the-monster.html
This site gives a short, simple character analysis of Frankenstein's monster—a surprisingly complex character given that he doesn't even actually have a name!

Video

The Real Story of Frankenstein's Monster—Full Documentary
www.youtube.com/watch?v=Biv0jp7CUtg.
This 82-minute 2014 BBC documentary tells the story behind the myth of Frankenstein's monster.

Bibliography

Bevington, Linda K., and CBHD research staff. "An Overview of Stem Cell Research." The Center for Bioethics & Human Dignity. August 2009. Retrieved August 19, 2015. http://cbhd.org/stem-cell-research/overview.

Dickson, Caitlin. "Creepy Stories of Grave Robbing." *Daily Beast*. January 20, 2013. http://www.thedailybeast.com/articles/2013/01/20/creepy-stories-of-grave-robbing.html.

European Graduate School, The. "Mary Shelley – Biography." Retrieved August 19, 2015. http://www.egs.edu/library/mary-shelley/biography.

Green, Treye. "Frankenstein Day: Five Myths About the 'Frankenstein' Monster." International Business Times. August 30, 2013. http://www.ibtimes.com/frankenstein-day-five-myths-about-frankenstein-monster-1402033.

History Embalmed. "Tomb Robbers." Retrieved August 19, 2015. http://www.historyembalmed.org/egyptian-tombs/tomb-robbers.htm.

Lammie, Rob. "Worth More Dead Than Alive: 5 Famous Grave Robberies." *Mental Floss*. November 4, 2009. http://mentalfloss.com/article/23184/worth-more-dead-alive-5-famous-grave-robberies.

Mayo Clinic Research. "About Regenerative Medicine." Retrieved August 19, 2015. http://www.mayo.edu/research/centers-programs/center-regenerative-medicine/patient-care/about-regenerative-medicine.

Norton Anthology of English Literature, The. "The Gothic: Overview." Retrieved August 19, 2015. http://www.wwnorton.com/college/english/nael/romantic/topic_2/welcome.htm.

Shelley, Mary Wollstonecraft. *Frankenstein; or, The Modern Prometheus*. Retrieved August 19, 2015. http://www.gutenberg.org/files/84/84-h/84-h.htm.

Index

Page numbers in **boldface** are illustrations. Entries in **boldface** are glossary terms.

About the Author

Cathleen Small is an editor and author. She has written numerous books for Cavendish Square. She studied the Gothic novel in college and loves a good creepy story! When she's not reading and writing, Cathleen can be found spending time with her two young sons and introducing them to the mythical world of Harry Potter.